American Indian Homes

TEPEES

by Jack Manning

CAPSTONE PRESS
a capstone imprint

First Facts are published by Capstone Press,
1710 Roe Crest Drive, North Mankato, Minnesota 56003
www.capstonepub.com

Library of Congress Cataloging-in-Publication Data
Manning, Jack.
  Tepees / by Jack Manning.
      pages cm. — (First facts. American Indian homes)
  Includes bibliographical references and index.
  Summary: "Informative, engaging text and vivid photos introduce readers to tepees"—
Provided by publisher.
  Audience: Grades K—3.
  ISBN 978-1-4914-0316-7 (library binding)
  ISBN 978-1-4914-0320-4 (paperback)
  ISBN 978-1-4914-0324-2 (eBook PDF)
  1. Tipis—Juvenile literature. I. Title.
  E98.D8M35 2015
  392.3'60899708—dc23   2014008077

Editorial Credits
Brenda Haugen, editor; Kyle Grenz, designer; Jo Miller, media researcher;
Kathy McColley, production specialist

Photo Credits
Bridgeman Art Library: Newberry Library, Chicago, Illinois, USA/American Photographer,
17; Cartesia, 6 (map); Corbis, 15, Bettmann, 7, Blue Lantern Studio, 13, National Geographic
Society/W. Langdon Kihn, 21, Robert Holmes, 9, Underwood & Underwood, 19; Getty
Images: Archive Photos/Buyenlarge, 11, Gallo Images/Danita Delimont, 5; Shutterstock:
aragami12345s, 1, ChameleonsEye, Cover, Heiko Kueverling, 3

Design Elements
Shutterstock: OHishiapply, s duffett, Tyler Olson

Printed in the United States of America in North Mankato, Minnesota.
042014   008087CGF14

Table of Contents

Chapter 1

What Is a Tepee?

Tepees are cone-shaped tents once used as homes. Tepees were made with wooden poles and buffalo **hides**. When buffalo became hard to find, people used **canvas** cloth instead.

Tepees were made in various sizes. Most were as tall as a one-story building. People often built tepees about 14 feet (4.3 meters) high and 13 feet (4 m) around.

> **hide**—the skin of an animal
>
> **canvas**—a type of strong cloth

Chapter 2

Who Lived in Tepees?

Some Plains Indian **tribes** lived in tepees. The tribes lived on the Great Plains of central North America. Most tepees were home to single families.

Tepees were good homes for life on the plains. They offered shelter from rain and snow. They were also easy to move.

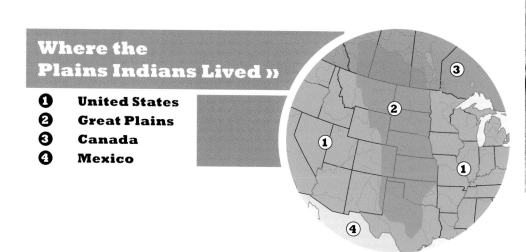

Where the Plains Indians Lived »

1. United States
2. Great Plains
3. Canada
4. Mexico

FACT

Today Plains Indians live in modern houses. But tribes still build and use tepees for ceremonies.

tribe—a group of people who share the same ancestors, customs, and laws

ceremony—formal actions, words, and often music performed to mark an important occasion

Chapter 3

Gathering Materials

Plains Indians used wooden poles for tepee **frames**. For each tepee, men cut down about 15 young pine trees. They removed the branches and bark from the trunk to make poles. Buffalo hides covered the tepee frame.

Women gathered dried grass and brush to fill tepee **liners**. The liners hung from the inside poles of the tepee. The filled liners helped keep the tepee warm.

Plains Indians hunted buffalo.

frame—the structure of a tepee

liner—animal skins or pieces of canvas sewn together to line the bottom half of a tepee

Chapter 4

Preparing the Materials

Women treated the buffalo hides. They cleaned off the hair and removed the fat. They soaked the hides in water to soften them. Then the hides were stretched on racks to dry.

Women sewed the dried hides together with buffalo **sinew**. They cut a door opening and sewed smoke flaps near the top of the cover.

A woman cleans a hide.

sinew—a strong piece of body tissue that connects muscle to bone

Building a Tepee

Women carefully built the tepee. They tied three poles together to form a **tripod**. They added thinner poles to make a cone-shaped frame. They wrapped the cover around the frame. Wooden stakes held the cover to the ground. Women also attached poles to the smoke flaps. People used the poles to close the flaps during rain and wind.

tripod—a stand with three legs

Poles formed a cone shape under the buffalo hide.

FACT
Small sticks called lacing pins closed the door opening.

Chapter 6

Inside a Tepee

Tepees were comfortable homes. People cooked, ate meals, and slept on furs and blankets. Families talked, sewed, and welcomed visitors in tepees. During the day, light shone through the smoke hole and door. At night, a fire warmed everyone inside. The smoke rose through the smoke hole to the outside.

People gather in a tepee.

Chapter 7

Tepee Villages

Plains Indians lived in villages. During the warm months, tepees often formed a circle. During the winter, villages were not shaped like circles. In cold weather the people camped along rivers.

The middle of the village was special. People held ceremonies there. Important people set up their tepees close to the center of the village.

FACT

Tepee doors faced east to the rising sun.

A tepee village stands near a river.

Chapter 8

Special Tepees

Large tepees had special uses. A council lodge often was set up near the middle of the village. Tribal leaders held meetings in the large lodge.

Some tepees had special decorations. Plains Indians sometimes painted their tepees. They painted animals, stars, and other designs on tepees.

Chapter 9

Moving Tepees

Plains Indians did not stay in one place. They moved when the seasons changed. Hunters followed the moving animal herds.

When they moved, Plains Indians took apart their tepees. They put their tepees and other belongings on a **travois**. Dogs or horses pulled the travois.

Amazing but True

The Saamis Tepee is the world's largest tepee. It was built for the 1988 Calgary Winter Olympics in Canada. It stands more than 20 stories tall. The tepee can handle winds of up to 150 miles (241 kilometers) per hour.

travois

travois—a frame that is shaped like a triangle and is used to move belongings

21

Glossary

canvas (KAN-vuhss)—a type of strong cloth

ceremony (SER-uh-moh-nee)—formal actions, words, and often music performed to mark an important occasion

frame (FRAYM)—the structure of a tepee

hide (HIDE)—the skin of an animal

liner (LINE-ur)—animal skins or pieces of canvas sewn together to line the bottom half of a tepee

sinew (SIN-yoo)—a strong piece of body tissue that connects muscle to bone

travois (truh-VOY)—a frame that is shaped like a triangle and is used to move belongings

tribe (TRIBE)—a group of people who share the same ancestors, customs, and laws

tripod (TRYE-pod)—a stand with three legs

Read More

Fitzgerald, Michael Owen. *Children of the Tipi: Life in the Buffalo Days.* Bloomington, Ind.: Wisdom Tales, 2013.

O'Hara, Megan. *Plains Communities Past and Present.* Who Lived Here? North Mankato, Minn.: Capstone Press, 2014.

Santella, Andrew. *Plains Indians.* First Nations of North America. Chicago: Heinemann Library, 2012.

Internet Sites

FactHound offers a safe, fun way to find Internet sites related to this book. All of the sites on FactHound have been researched by our staff.

Here's all you do:

Visit *www.facthound.com*

Type in this code: 9781491403167

Check out projects, games and lots more at
www.capstonekids.com

Index

Critical Thinking Using the Common Core

1. Did weather affect tepee villages? How were the villages different in the winter and summer? (Key Ideas and Details)

2. Look at the Fact box on page 11. What is the author trying to say? Did women soften hides in other ways? If so, how? (Integration of Knowledge and Ideas)